Return To Sender

A Book of Poetry, Prose, and Otherwise Unsent Letters

Alice Allis

While there is no direct mention of subjects' names, the author can only hope that any resemblance to persons alive or dead be apparent to them and those who know them. The author has avoided most names, in general, for privacy purposes. All events described herein are from the perspective of the author's personal experience, with minimal liberties taken for the creative writing word vomit. In the end, this is a memoir, if you squint and tilt your head a little. Haters, and the author will hold your hand while they say this, can piss right off.

To request permission, contact the publisher at aliceallisofficial@gmail.com

ISBN: 979-8-218-43761-9 (paperback)
ISBN: 979-8-218-47470-6 (e-book)

Library of Congress Control Number: 2024914930

First Edition October 13th, 2024

Editing by Emily Fredericksen
Cover Design by Samantha Sanderson-Marshall
Illustrations by Alice Allis
Photography by Alice Allis
Photo of Author by Alice Allis
Photo Appearances: Alice Allis, Rebecca Allis, Ivie Allis

Published by Alice Allis
Colorado Springs, CO

Instagram: @AliceAllisOfficial

No men were harmed in the writing of this book.
(I was told I have to say that for legal purposes.)

Trigger Warning:

Some language, topics, and images might be sensitive in nature including, but not limited to, those pertaining to sexual activities, suicide and self-harm, emotional and verbal abuse, and – overall – dating men.

Reader discretion is advised.

For anyone who has ever dated a Brad, Chad, or Ryan:
may the Universe forever feed them what Karma serves up,
and grace you with greatness.

To my loves:

Speak in understatements,
write in reality,
daydream in exaggerations.

With all I have,
Alice

Preface

Since I was much younger than I am now, I have been told I was a good writer. Writing has always been the easiest way to express my emotions and experiences. The written word is, and always has been, the most ideal form of expression for myself. I have used writing to apologize, provide praise and gratitude, criticize and condemn, and share my love with others.

While I have considered publishing my poetry, prose, and letters for quite some time, this always felt like the dream of a much younger version of me. *Return To Sender* was never what I had ever intended when thinking about publishing poetry. I had been collecting my pieces for several years, often hidden away within locked documents whose passwords had been long forgotten. This collection of works came about when I had returned to the art form after ending an engagement.

My former lover became angry that he was no longer the knight in shining armor that I had once seen him as and had since revealed himself to be destructive and manipulative. He had spent months shaming and speaking ill of me to all his loved ones, while continuing to solicit sexual encounters from me and keeping our interactions secret from current partners. So, when written pieces reflecting this evolved understanding of him had been shared to my social media, he became upset. Even though only he and I would be able to recognize it was about him, I was still condemned. I scrubbed my social media of all written works going back over a decade. After my sister and best friend talked me to my senses, I dug around my mind to get the passwords to old pieces. Within a month, I had not only found all the old pieces I had written, but also wrote over one hundred new pieces. I have since narrowed down what is shared to the book you now hold in your hands.

Needless to say, this has been a passion project: one of rage and resentment, but also one of self-discovery and self-love. This is a love letter to myself. No matter how foolish my decision making has been within relationships, I have truly learned to recognize my value, and how to prioritize my self-worth before others. I'm never one to avoid topics of mental health, so I don't mind the vulnerable experience of publishing my experiences of coming to terms with my anxious attachment style and truly just wanting to be loved for who I am instead of a person others project onto me.

This book is separated into four parts. Part One is inspired by the first time I lived in Seattle, circa 2014. Part Two is a direct continuation from Part One, as the given section is inspired by my return to North Carolina in 2015. Part Three is inspired by my return to Seattle in 2021 and is directly followed by Part Four. Part Four is inspired by the end of the engagement and my healing process since.

My writing style is raw, not shying away from topics of sex, self-harm, and suicidal ideation. For all those who might be experiencing thoughts of self-harm or suicide, or find themselves in a crisis, I highly encourage reaching out to a loved one or even the National Suicide Prevention Lifeline (800-273-8255 or 988).

Finally, I would like to share that I have no intent on keeping the financial gains produced from this book. This project was never to pay bills. Just as this writing experience has assisted in healing me, I would like to push that into the world – A pay it forward of sorts. For more information about the direction of funding, I encourage you to follow my social media.

Return To Sender

A Book of Poetry, Prose, and Otherwise Unsent Letters

A Cycle

My memories fall like raindrops on the street of life – no particular order or path in time. Just memories into tears, tears into words. Words now ink the paper of what once stood tall, similar to how I once stood tall until I had my fall from a plateau of what I thought was love. It turns out I had taken the wrong path, and the cliff was only loneliness and self-hatred. The storm of my sorrow now releases each moment as though a child's hand plummets into a bushel of berries to find the best one. A mess erupts with stained hands. While I enjoy what is left of me, all that was bruised and crushed leaks out, finding its way back to the soil where it came from.

Finding Old Pieces

I rediscovered old pieces
with distasteful memories
of people I no longer know,
relieved I have grown past
such foolish times of wishing
for outcomes to be different.

Part One

Hopeless Romantic

I live life walking a thin line
stretched between two towers.
I always seem to be one step away
from falling in love or breaking my heart.

Hope

When I look into your eyes,
I see my universe expanding;
for what I once knew as small
has grown with each moment.

Wishing

My dear, I wish for you.
All I want is this to come true.
If nothing else is to be,
might I have you?

Natural

Your lips move on mine
like air moves in my lungs
or blood fills my heart.
It's such a natural feeling
I wonder how I have lived life
this long without you.

Orion's Downfall

I look to Orion
as though he could
actually grant me
my many wishes;
though I already know,
deep within my heart,
you are more
than he could provide.

Held Back

The words I wish to say
are contained behind a cell of teeth,
escaping only in my mind
when we are held close together.

Speechless

Speechless.

That is how I am left when he speaks to me. I don't know how to respond to the cute gestures, or the sweet words that dance off his tongue, waltz through his teeth, and slow dance their way to my ears. They go straight to my brain, where they continue as a jumbled mess of a house party. They disrupt my centered mind, breaking down the barriers as though they were only walls of twigs. I am dazed by the word play. I stumble from happiness and fall for him over and over again. I try to pick myself up from the disorder I am left in. Over thinking everything – all the words spoken and read; all of the dances hosted in my head – he only continues to prove that I don't need those barriers.

Flustered.

That is how I become when I know I need to respond, but the words won't flow, the fingers won't type, and the mind is still hung on his words. I stare at the message on the screen or the look in his eye. I am stunned by the coy shrug of his shoulders as he tries to make himself the size that I am actually feeling. I am paralyzed by the bashful grin, which parts his lips enough for him to playfully stick out the tip of his tongue. He questions my stare, my smile, and my longing eyes. I respond with nothing; sipping on a drink before quickly asking a question to divert his curiosity of my infatuation.

Breathless.

I stop breathing the moment his lips interlock with mine. My eyes closed, hand on his cheek, his arms wrapped around me in a hugging embrace. In that moment our bodies defy physics as we continue to move against each other. My mind goes blank. There are no thoughts, only actions. I would be okay if we were locked in this moment until the end if time itself. When our lips detach, I stare back into his eyes; the cycle begins over.

He leaves me speechless.

You Go First

I need you to be
the first to utter the words
I have feared speaking.

The Conductor

Your voice conducts
a symphony of emotions
all with a simple whisper
and a wave of your hand
against my bare skin.

Moonlight

Fingers pressed against keys,
As my favorite song plays.
His memory surpassed mine.

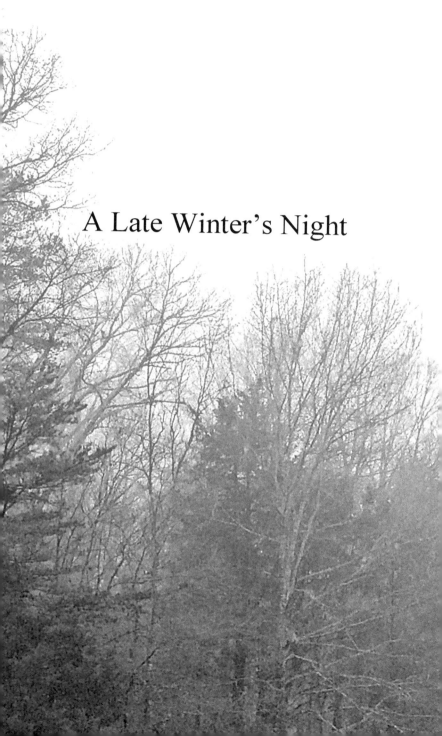

A Late Winter's Night

The late afternoon's rain droplets seep into my jeans, absorbed by the pressure of my body resting on the wooden bench. The aroma of blossoming flowers from a local store front takes lift on the back of a soft breeze. The path ahead of me is lit with bulbs weaved into the bare tree branches. A rapid pitter-patter of water from a nearby fountain harmonizes with the sound of people passing by. It's hard to believe this to be winter, with the warmth of spring.

I sit in wait for you to accompany me. My hands were buried in the pockets of my flannel jacket, and my arms held ridged against my torso in an attempt to stay a little warmer. I watch as a pair walks past, discussing the movie that had just been completed only moments earlier. I pretend to be invisible: I don't want to be seen; I just want to observe the world. I want to experience the view of a great narrator until you break the silence and bring me back to a shared moment where I am a participant.

Disjointed

You asked me why I love you,
to which I pulled out a list.
I asked you why you love me,
but there was only silence.

Not For Me

He whispered words
of love into my ear
before calling me
by another's name.

It's Hard to Forget

I imagine his lips on yours,
All the while yours glide across mine.
The thought fills me with jealousy,
A feeling I can't deny.

Fatigue

Your lies have caught up to you.
My energy has failed me,
and my legs grow weak.
The ones who win this race
Are the ones who never contended.

Missing Seattle

His words pierced my heart,
slaughtering all the exaggerated hope of
what I had imagined we would have become.

Discernment

I fear the dark
because its lies
seem all too true.

Salvage

His anger showered the kitchen
like that of an avalanche
let loose on the cupboards of antiques.
I shifted through the debris
scattered across three rooms
only able to salvage one plate.

Anatomy of Fear

It courses through your veins, pumped from your tattered heart; an organ only glued together with the crystallized tears of your pain caused by all processors. Powered by distrust, it surges between vitals, looping around the track of limbs, to begin racing throughout the second half of the hidden tunnels. Energized by each weak heartbeat.

You inhale rejection and lies, but exhale hesitation. Reciprocity constricts the muscles, paralyzing every muscle with the venom before ingesting you whole. You take faster, yet shallow breaths, in hopes that you'll soon discover anything other than toxin.

The choke hold of betrayal suffocates the brain. Your actions are blurred with tears as you melt into the floor; marrow turned to adrenaline just to prolong the complete collapse of existence. What is left is a puddle of a former self enveloped in darkness.

The words of pure sincerity inflate your lungs with the fear that originally dematerialized. A body brought back to life, only to be manipulated by what destroyed it. Scars of distrust and anxiety leave you handcuffed, imprisoned by your own insecurities.

Repetition, the waters of time stream across your hard body, wearing it down until the fever breaks. Having had the time for reality to defend against instinct; the war waged, mind against soul. A battle on the field of an uncontrolled element, only causing self-deprivation until the necessary victor conquered the untamed beast, which invaded like an invisible virus through the wounds of a broken heart.

Deception

He is a dark knight of destruction - a vigilante of her heart - eradicating her numbness with chaos and agony, tormenting a spellbound mind with an illusion of love all while serenading her with a soulmate's lullaby: manipulating all of her emotions, blinding her of the bruises.

Subtle Requests

Sometimes,
When I cry for help
It sounds like a greeting.

Helium

All hope drifts away, floating out the window with one
deciding moment, scattering amongst the clouds like a
bouquet of balloons let loose into the fierce wind.

I watch it quickly evaporate, becoming one with the horizon;
I continue to hope for more than just an illusion of the mind
making sense of chaos.

Disgrace

My mind tells me I'm covered in filth. Your words, your touch, your intentions: they fill me with disgrace. I've tried to scrub myself clean, though the sight of blood-stained water prevents me from continuing. I pretend not to notice the lingering thoughts and try to distract myself from being consumed by a presence that is only imagined.

Empty Jars

Loving you was like hunting for fireflies: I spent most of my time alone, in the dark, tracking small moments of sudden light. Eventually I learned it was best to let someone else find your beauty.

Delusions

You told me who you were, and I didn't believe you. You showed me with your actions, and I turned a blind eye. I fought you and my gut believed there was more worth to you than you thought. Once I couldn't breathe anymore from your abuse is when I finally realized I should have listened.

A Desire to Read

You were like a good book:
I was sad when it was over,
not because I missed you,
but because it was not real.

A daily reminder for myself:
my fairy tale won't be a book
to be placed on a shelf when finished,
but an actual person to be cherished.

The Platform

He stood on the platform with a certain type of confidence; one that tried to overcompensate for the insecurities which were etched deep into the lines of his face. Trying to keep composure as every worry for the next three weeks rushed through his brain. He had no choice in the matter; the dorms were closed for the break, and the flight was already paid for. Last minute scenarios of how he could avoid the inevitable flashed behind his eyelids with every blink, each one being more outrageously unlikely than the previous. Maybe the train to the airport would derail; preferably before he stepped on to it... Or maybe if he was on it, the death of a train crash would be more bearable than dealing with the dysfunction and everything that would come up during the time with his family.

The next train will arrive in two minutes.
Please stand behind the yellow line.

He looked down at his feet. His right foot was right on the line. It was this moment that he realized just how close to the edge of the platform he actually was. The idea of being that close scared him, but then thinking to himself, he reasoned that it was no less scary than the scenarios he had just been imagining. He stared at the thick yellow line that bordered the edge of the platform. There was nothing on his mind; no thought, no words, nothing. Just the image of the lines he was staring at. It wasn't until the front of the train had rushed past him that he realized he had zoned out. Looking up, he watched as the train slowed, and eventually stopped. The doors opened, directly in front of him. He stood still for a second as people poured into the train car around him. Finally, he stepped onto the train, finding a seat to himself. He stared out the window.

Flight

You clipped my wings before requesting that I fly us into the distance, only to become enraged that I couldn't lift us off the ground. You caged me in shame by your lectures of blame, guilting me into thinking I could only fly again if I trust your shearing hands. My spirit is that of wilderness and chaos, and I plotted to be unbound from your bars of darkness. I released myself from your hold. You never realized until it was too late. I had grown my feathers back and saw through your secret combination to be released. I am one with the air, with freedom, and you will forever be trapped in your own shadow, as you no longer have hold over me.

Leaving the Emerald City

By the time I escaped,
I had gained a heart,
though it was broken;
cultivated a brain,
yet still very naive;
gained the courage to leave,
but not to face my fears;
and managed to acquire
a one-way ticket
back to the last place
I thought I would run to.

No Postage Needed

My thoughts of you
have become friends
with the delete button.

Going unseen is safer
than you twisting them
into your mind's pleasure.

Faded Scars

You have become nothing
more than the indentation
marked against my skin,
the same ones I pray will one day
vanish like you eventually did.

Lesson on Regret

It is a frozen tundra
whose winds stir blizzards
of materialized unease
and walls of icy mirrors
mimicking past decisions.
If transfixed too long,
your past becomes
future regrets.

Part Two

Follow the Leader

His leap was my reason
ten digits were inscribed
on a piece of scrape paper
as I followed his example.

New Life

I was an autumn spirit
birthed in the summer;
you were my spring
who found me in a dark winter.

Coin

Reality and imaginary:
two sides of the same coin,
and I'm confused,
which side is you.

All Day, Until Five

Listening to our playful banter -
the way it makes us laugh,
the grin etched into his face -
brings a joy I hope to never lose.

Mesmerized

I find myself lost in the gaze of your brown eyes. At face value they look like the eyes of an average twenty something, but once I stare long enough, I can see just the contrary. Your eyes are those of someone far older than the young body which currently possesses them; they are eyes of someone who has seen the world, and the unfortunate pain that follows witness to tragedy. Though your posture and words tell a very diluted story of such travels, your eyes share the true tales.

I blindly search through your memories as though attempting to read a picture book of two-dimensional braille. Trying to see even just a glimpse of those past realities, I dive deeper and deeper. My trance is broken at the sound of you clearing your throat. You smile kindly as I blush; I hope you don't realize how lost in those orbs I am. You continue speaking, and while I am not stuck deep within your gaze, I am deep in thought. How could something so pained and dilapidated be so beautiful?

I've heard it said that the eyes are the window to the mind and soul. Your mind is elegantly gorgeous, and soul painstakingly beautiful, as though the scars of misfortune were of natural design, as opposed to being inflicted. While I know you will share all in due time, I want to discover such delicacies on my own: a hunt for lost treasure, a challenge very few would even think about attempting. I want to explore all I can to understand how to love you for more than the shell protecting an old soul.

Coffee Shoppe

For many years now,
I have been waiting
for something wonderful
to walk into my life.
I ponder this thought
over a cup of hot chai
while at a table for two.
You sit down in front of me,
and I realized that you had
walked in a long time ago.

Cold Comfort

We make a bed
under a starry night,
though miles apart,
this is no plight;
we find cold comfort
with the cosmos' flight.

Sorcery

What magic is this
that you can tame
my anxious heart
with such soothing words?

Still Alive

If you tear past the scars
you will find it still beats.
If you listen long enough
it will hum your name.

Sweet Healer

You picked up the pieces, sewing them together stitch by stitch. You grafted tissues into this cavity, regrowing what was once ripped from me. Your arms bandaged this tattered shell, incubating a damaged soul.

Mystical Medicine

With a simple kiss
this tattered and shattered heart
was healed of its wounds.

Spring

My love:
a frozen paradise;
the more you hold me,
the faster I thaw.

Subtleties

I have laid breadcrumbs
hoping for you to follow
the trail back to me.

In Due Time

I shared all my desires with you
except for a mere two;
you'll have to search my gaze
a little longer before I submit,
for there are three words
I cannot bring myself to speak.

Secrets

He read the messages
hidden within my words,
pointing them out with
inquisitive tones
as I plead the fifth to
his curious accusations.

Affection

Oh my dear,
draw me near.
Let me peer
into those eyes.
Is it not clear,
that this is more
than just a mere
affection.

Sacred Fruit

You have grown tall
within my heart,
baring the best fruit
I long to taste.

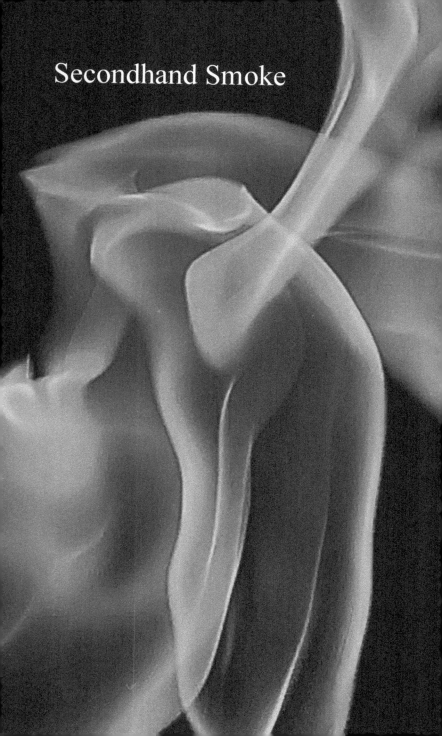
Secondhand Smoke

His kiss was intoxicating. Full of passionate longing as our lips moved against one another. Our tongues danced like long lost partners, seeing the other for the first time in ages; stumbling and staggering within the other's mouth. The harsh taste of smoke tingled as though it was peppermint. I couldn't get enough. My breathing became heavy with lust for more. Though the experience ended, I was left with your scent of cigarettes and whisky to linger on my breath for the drive home. While the late-night affair can never be repeated, I sometimes search for your aftertaste in those of others.

Like It's The Last Time

I attempt to remember
every possible moment
because I fear you will turn
into nothing more than
a mirage of happiness.

When You're Next to Me

Thoughts of you send shivers of anxiety surging though my body - a rolling wave capsizing all rational thought, while an impossible hope is brought to the surface, bubbling in the surf of broken concepts as I talk myself out of saying anything too rash.

Midnight Thoughts

It's almost midnight, and the only thing keeping me awake is the thought of you... Okay! That's a lie. There are the sleep-induced grunts of those around me. There is the gentle, yet comforting breeze. There is the crackling sound of the fire slowly burning out. There is the hum of the insects. The only thing on my mind is you though. I lay here wondering if you softly grunt in your slumber or if you would ever be sleeping close enough for me to hear you. I'm curious if we would ever cuddle near a crackling fire. Just you and I sitting beside a fireplace, a shared blanket wrapped around us. I would rest my head on your shoulder as the embers glowed, and shadows danced across your features. The next morning, your soft hum would wake me. I'd grunt sleepily as you smiled at my pathetic attempt to wake up. Alas, it is almost midnight, and my mind continues to wander to distant thoughts and imagined scenarios.

Time Froze

There we were: standing on the back porch, surrounded by the void of night. The orbs of gas and fire dusted the sky above, as Orion kept watch. I could barely make out your silhouette as we stood only inches apart, but I could feel your presence. I felt safe; at the same time, I could feel a hurricane of anxiety beginning to rage in the pit of my stomach, making its way along the organs of my chest cavity. In only a split second, it hit land, wreaking havoc on my heart as we began to say our goodbyes and good nights. Right before you turned away from me, there was a moment that you leaned closer, our foreheads almost touching. Part of me wanted to jump at the chance. I wanted nothing else; the other part anchored me, holding me grounded. The moment you turned away, a surge broke all the levies. I watched as that silhouette began to fade into the abyss. My heart sank into the treacherous currents, drowning as the water rose. The only thought that passed through my head was 'there goes my chance.'

I always let the moment pass like sand falling through the fingers of an open hand, an hourglass of every moment missed. I stared at my feet, disappointed, yet again, that I was defeated by my own guard – a prisoner within the self-built walls around me. The sound of your foot landing on wood was like a hundred nails against the slate of a chalkboard: it was physically painful to hear. I wasn't going to lose this chance; I couldn't let this moment slip away. Now, a new storm of adrenaline and determination gained momentum. A perfect storm waged war, it was now or never. Before you could get too far, I leaned forward, stretching to grab something: a hand, an arm, a sleeve. My fingers glided across the fabric of your shirt, but not enough for me to grab ahold of you. Luckily, you stopped moving and turned back to me. Stepping forward, I pressed off my heels just to stand a little taller. I saw a small glint in your eye when I laid my hand gently against your cheek.

In a quick motion, our faces were touching. My eyes closed as tightly as I could squeeze them shut. I feared if I was to open them then you would vanish, and the memory of tonight would disappear like a dream when woken up, only to become a disillusioned blur of fantasy to daydream about. In that moment, I could not feel the motion of time. It was like the universe stopped expanding, the earth's spin slowed, and all the cosmos watched as you slipped your hands between my shirt and jacket. Wrapping both arms around me, your fingertips met on my spine. Slowly, and ever so gently, they traveled down to the small of my back, where they found their resting spot. We reluctantly settled back into reality. The universe continued expanding, the earth spun at its normal speed around the sun, and time moved right past us. I felt accomplished, for in that moment I broke away from being transfixed within an emotional swell, and with an audience of little lights twinkling above.

Little Meeting Rooms

Home is relative
to my proximity to you.
Yesterday it was
in a coffee house;
a sushi restaurant
the night before.
One day I hope for it
to be a place of our own.
Until then, home is
the rooms we meet in.

Dazed

We bundle close
as the sun sets low
in the western sky,
imagining a day
we will eventually drive
into its blazed glory.

Let Us

Let us wake up early in the morning, before the dawn's fog has settled, cruising to the likes of the '90s and savoring hot tea. The horizon, a powder blue, swirls like a child's artwork with pink clouds, and a black, cratered road stretching for miles. Each bump is covered by your voice echoing the radio as mine is silent, but my lips still move to hide the obvious fact that I can't really sing.

Let us get lost in the wilderness, hiking over fallen trees and across little creeks, pretending to be explorers in a faraway land. The strong scent of pine and damp wood fill the air while birds who hide amongst the foliage chirp out of time with the crunch of our feet on gravel. I run ahead until my wheezing becomes too much; hunched over, looking up I see you jogging in place, that grin of victory matched with my breathless laugh.

Let us slowly dance outside as the thunder cracks, and the water pitter-patters on our shoulders, before eventually seeking shelter under the large oak tree. Droplets fall from the leaves above, dampening our clothes to even more uncomfortable levels, proving just how irrational of a place it was to hide. When the storm finally passes, we continue to trail blaze the inevitable loop leading us back to civilization.

Let us cuddle in front of the fireplace, binging our favorite movie series, stealing glances as the other pretends not to notice. The entertainment becomes background noise to a silent conversation of smirks and playful glares as our legs continuously pretzel together. We tease with noses touching, challenging the other to move first, but our game eventually ends unrewarded.

Let us fall asleep snuggled close to each other, filling the silence with our dozing sighs, dreaming of what the future holds. The fan creates a gentle breeze, causing me to nestle closer to you, curled in what will later be a regrettable position. You turn over so our noses touch once again, except there is no challenge this time; we connect gently before giving in to the night.

Side Conversation

I undress you with my eyes
As you sit across from me.
I imagine each button undone
while your lips press against my skin.
I sip my coffee to hide
the grin drawn on my face,
since the conversation I want
is best had in bed.

New Territory

Rediscover a land
known only to few;
explore regions untouched
by your searching hands;
adventure past my hips,
all while entertaining my lips.

That One Time

In one quick movement our bodies were connected in ways like that of the earth meeting the ocean: two entities within one being. No natural disaster could even compare to the combination of the two of us together. The earthquake of my body rocking his, and his tongue a tsunami of energy between my lips. Both earth and water settled before either could conquer the other, but only linger as companions.

Basking in the entanglement of each other's presence, our lungs filled before traveling hemispheres to finish the dance. As the dance came to an end, the earth surrounded the ocean with a grip that not even heaven could have broken. Ending perfectly the way things began: like vines tangled together. The earth and water rested.

Late Night Joys

The soft glow of the overhead lamp gently lit the studio with a light like that of the early morning sun as it creeps above the horizon. Insomnia was tonight's companion as I sat on the couch with a book in hand. I held it up in front of my face as though to shield myself from distractions of the apartment, but at this time of night the only distractions were internal. I would be in the middle of a paragraph, then find myself in deep thought. Occasionally, I would glance over to the bed to make sure I had not woken you with the light of the lamp, the turning of the page, or the involuntary humored exhale at various situations of this novel. It was at the sound of the creaking bed when I realized you had woken from the peaceful slumber, which I previously had left you in before retiring to the opposite side of the room.

I watched as you sluggishly activated your phone, checking the time before sitting still, perplexed that you were the only one in bed. I laughingly wished you a good morning, resting my arms on the back of the couch in an offering gesture for you to join me. Wrapping the comforter around yourself, you shuffled lethargically across the room, and sat down next to me. You said nothing out of what I assumed to be sheer exhaustion or not being fully awake. You placed your head on my shoulder as I bookmarked the paperback and placed it on the makeshift coffee table. Leaning against me, I wrapped my arms around you, and kissed the top of your head, apologizing for having woken you.

You adjust your body, laying your head on my lap and curling up to fit within the restraints of the couch. You gave me a sleepy nod and smile when I asked if you were comfortable. Looking down at you, I could feel nothing but the utmost joy of being in your presence. I grinned and let out a humored huff. I lower my head to yours, kissing you good night one more time. I gently ran my hand over your head; within only a matter of minutes you had been overcome by your heavy eyelids. As your breathing slowed, and my own eyelids became difficult to hold open, I whispered my love for you. We spent the rest of the night sleeping on that couch, with your head on my lap.

Morning Eyes

You hold me tighter than
I have ever been held.
As though you fear my form
to truly be mere vapors,
only to be fade away like a
dream cloud upon waking;
yet, every morning, I am still
in your arms and I am dazzled
by the relief in your eyes.

Love's Truth

Only the ignorant
would say they loved
each other as brothers,
for we truly know
they were far closer.

Don't Let Go

The rays of the late afternoon sun beat down, slightly warming the skin that is still bare; while the autumn breeze glides gracefully across the surface of the lake's low tide, meeting my body, and forcing me to cross my arms in an attempt to focus all my body heat to one central location. I lean against the railing of the pier, resting my arms - still held tight against my chest - on top of it. I smile as the wind kisses my cheek; closing my eyes, I slightly tilt my head back, absorbing all there is to take in. The smell of fallen leaves after they had changed from green to the multitudes of reds and browns, the lapsing water against the shore as aquatic foliage dries in the sun light, and then something a little muskier: an unnatural smell only created by that of some department store. The vibrations of your footsteps travel through the old wood, shaking the railing. The sound becomes a little louder with each transaction of shoe against the rickety pier before the noise ceases completely.

Only moving my head, I glance over my left shoulder: I don't see you though. A look of confusion paints over the smirk that had once shaped my mouth. Just when I turn to look back at the setting sun as it's pulled below the lake, staining the sky effortlessly as it is forced to display a majestic masterpiece in other lands, your lips make contact with my neck. My breath catches as yours is released in small puffs against my collarbone. Wrapping your arms around my waist, you find the pockets of my jacket, slipping your hand inside. Leaning back against your chest, I use your shoulder as a pillow, resting as though it was time for bed. I stretch my arms out above us, reaching as far as I can. My stance of victory over a beautiful day brings a chuckle from within your throat. You lean into my ear and whisper: how is your soul?

My soul is good; it is very good.

Inevitable

Both hands are gripping the handle.
A trickle of blood glints against the silver,
As the blade pressed against my chest.

My dear Sir;
The choice is yours,
What will it be?
Shall I hand you my heart,
Or twist the dagger?

Either way I will feel the pain.
The blade will pierce this skin of mine.
It is inevitable.

A Promise Kept

In the end,
My mind may run dry,
My body may fall to pieces,
The world may implode,
But my words will never change.
They are for you;
No matter the fallout.

Balloon

My soul's nomadic tendencies are like an untethered balloon: randomly floating free and directionally challenged by the slightest of breezes.

Honesty

It would be a lie to say
loving is what I do best
because my love has
failed more times than
I would like to admit.

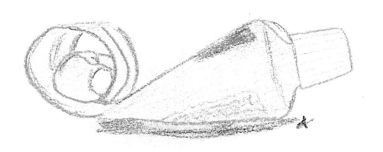

Super Glue

The silence is deafening. You said all you could remember from the hours of rehearsing to yourself. You practiced exactly what to say, how to say it, even the right moment to touch my hand as I stared into my coffee. I wonder to myself if it's possible to get a larger cup: I'm going to need it. Three shots of flavoring please. Oh, no! Not caramel, whisky would be nice. Thanks. The server walks away, confused why one boy is choking back tears as the other leans in to begin more whispering, attempting to not be too loud for the surrounding ears of the biblically entertained.

I trace the rim of the glass with a finger as I try to gather my thoughts, though I focus more on the loose grounds drowned at the bottom of the shallow murkiness. To be quite honest, I had a feeling something was wrong, or at least not right. Well, I guess right and wrong are only relative at this point. While this is wrong for me, it is right for you. Was it relative when we first kissed? Is it relative for my heart to be made of glue, and you just so happened to be nearby as I flung it to see where it would land. I know I have an awful aim, but maybe if it had hit a tree, I would be stopping the destruction of the park across the street instead of you bulldozing through the little cottage I built for us. It was a cozy little home, with the fireplace always ablaze, but I had just stepped through the threshold to a dark room, wall bare.

You sit at a table set for two, prepared to tell me of your future; a future without me. No, I stand corrected. A future with me, but only as a memory, or learning experience, whatever explanation is easiest for your conscious to accept. I was a steppingstone of emotions as you moved onto the next, I lay sunk in the ground. I wonder if that is how these coffee grounds felt as they sank to the bottom. My mind plays with these thoughts as it becomes more difficult not to cry. Each inhale is like another pump at the old well. I look up to see you staring at me as though waiting for me to ease your conscience. I can't fake this feeling; I've surpassed being able to draw on a smile to pretend it will all be alright.

The server returns with a refill for my cup, but at that moment it was too much for me to sit in the booth any longer. I push past her, aiming for the parking lot. I hurry in the best 'I'm upset, stay out of my way' walk I could perform. The brisk mountain air hits me hard as I push through the diner's doors. I look for my car, but remember I rode with you. I refuse to go back inside; I refuse to give you this moment. You just had yours, now it's my turn.

The statement I'm making is that I thought this meant more; I thought I meant more. I thought. Maybe I didn't think. I was so infused at the thought of even thinking of you. That glue dried fast - too fast. Now I was left in the gravel lot off the mountain road, crying over torn heart strings that had once been connected to you. I hear a bell behind me; I knew it was you walking out the door, and it was only confirmed with the double beep of your car unlocking. I climb into the passenger's seat and stare out the window as you pull onto the road to drive us home.

Wanderlust

I wished to hang a map upon the wall to play as a target. No specific destination, only the needle point of a dart can decide the mark. Though I know upon leaving, you'll be nowhere to be found, so I'll have to adventure on my own.

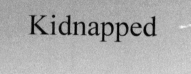

We traveled in opposite directions.
As you arrived at your destination,
I was already being dragged away
on an unexpected journey far from
the plans you and I made together.

Curious

Sometimes I wish
I could get a glimpse
of the ending,
just to see if you're
happier without me.

Metamorphosis

Your heart has seemed to have sprouted wings.
For it now flutters away on those gentle breezes –
the same ones that caress your cheek
as you stare out at the horizon.

The stale sunset painting the sky
orange and red is slowly conquered by a void of black
while the sun dips low, diving into the trenches
as though attempting to avoid the bullets of battle.

It's a bitter reminder to your war weary heart,
since it barely escaped the front lines,
having nursed each laceration,
forming a cocoon of insecurities and anxieties.

Your heart has since emerged;
words roll off your tongue
like the fine dust from your wings
As you drift away, migrating to new lands.

May you one day find your happiness
while exploring the many fields you travel;
though, always know it will come from within
and not from the external forces around you.

Part Three

A First Date

Clouds shield a couple's eyes
from star dust as it dances by.

A great stone table made a bed,
for this couple to rest their heads.

Arms wrapped tight around each other,
bodies held close just like old lovers.

This young couple lays in peace,
conversing without cease.

Two people embrace with a hold so tight,
bundled together for a long autumn night.

Fear

You asked me what my biggest fear was.
I responded with 'free falling…'
What I left out was '… in love with someone'.

Shock

The words seemed to flow so easily and elegantly from your lips. It was nothing to you, just your average compliment. Words of affirmation. Words of reassurance. They were everyday words one would think people heard often. They were foreign to my ears though. By the time my brain could register, the levies had already broke. Tears pooled under my eyes. Like midsummer's rain, the water was too much to hold back. Tears crashed to the ground. I could not comprehend why such words would be said to me. I had never associated any of them with anything about me.

We Move On

We each have accomplished
the world's task to destroy
our humanity, yet we both
still have strength to continue;
our conquering is far from over.

Blushing

It rushed from my heart
to my cheeks the moment
he confessed what I had
been holding back;
his kiss stained my lips
for a brief moment of time.

Frozen Treasure

I haven't experienced love like this before;
a snowflake in a world of water droplets
that sparkles with its own unique pattern.

Departures

It's an impending feeling of losing you, never to be seen after our good night wishes. Though our beds are separated by mere miles and promises hold hope captive for tomorrow, fear looms within my lingering thoughts of you. Before closing my eyes for a restless night's slumber, you are destined to haunt my dreams once sleep arrives.

Comfort Care

Face buried in the fabric of my shirt, now drenched with their tears. Their body convulsed with sorrow. They only needed to be held for a moment to know what had been missed: the tranquility of someone that even cared for a fraction of a moment, someone to listen to their grief. It was within that fraction that every emotion flooded to the surface. They felt as though they'd lost control of their body, and only needed my arms to hold them together again. Like new clay filling in the cracks of a broken vessel, they were whole again for just a little longer.

Skydiving

Falling for you was no accidental trip or even a slip,
but a full-on sprint and leap right off the edge.
A ledge that had been feared for it's unknown.
Now I fall past a point of no return with
hopes and dreams being my only parachute.
Reality's forces will determine if I survive this plunge.

If You Were Me

If you had my eyes,
you would see all
the wonder and beauty
I experience within you.

Little Hopes

Someday we will fall asleep together. We won't have to worry about one leaving as we'll stay tightly tangled in the other's limbs. For tonight, though, we are in our own beds. I dream of the next time I can fall asleep with you.

Long Nights

Sleep eludes the active mind,
leaving sanity to decipher
the brewed creations
of fantasy and reality.

Bedtime

Come be the reason for me to crawl into bed. This mattress only reminds me of all the lonely nights I wish I could happily live without.

Swaddle me like an infant in the blanket of your arms constricting me. Press your lips against me. Promise it will be alright.

Hush my restlessness with your breath against my ear, nuzzle your cheek to the back of my head; whisper those sweet nothings and draw me near.

Addiction

The line so expertly cut.
The needle so carefully placed.
The cocktail so artfully mixed.
The pill that's hard to swallow.
You're the addiction I suffer from,
Yet the one thing I'm unable to grasp.

Orbit

The moon cannot shine
without its sun,
just as I am nothing
more than a rock
floating through a void
without you.

Next Time

The next time you
have me in your arms,
hold me a little tighter;
the next time we kiss,
kiss me once more;
next time you fear rejection,
take that leap of faith -
I'll be right there to catch you.

Lay Claim

Claim this land:
it is rightfully yours;
for those who once laid claim
no longer hold control.
You have liberated
this captive soul.
You are now my king,
and I, your kingdom.

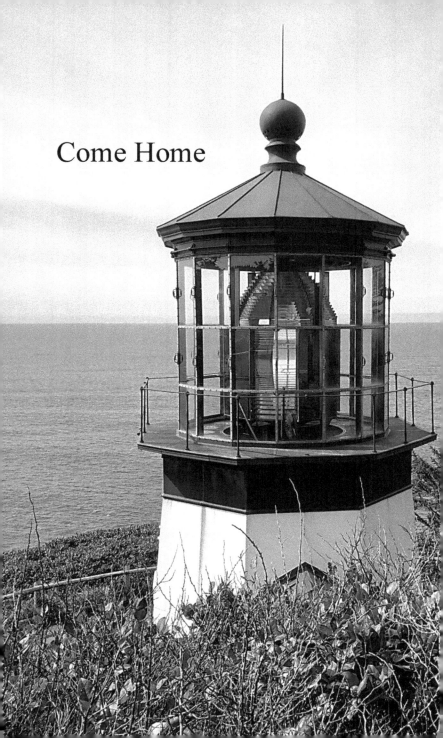

Come Home

Come into my arms,
for I shall be your shelter
from the raging storm.

Predictions

I don't fear falling in love with you.
I fear that you may fall out of love with me.

Fond Memory

His skin was soft against my cheek as I rested on his chest. Cheek on one pec while my hand rested peacefully on his right. The subtle sound of heartbeats echoed in my ear. Legs crisscrossed each other in an abstract form. One arm wrapped around my neck for a hand to rest upon my back; his other moved across my shoulder to form a tight embrace as his cheek rested on my head. A noticeable shift in desire - an urge previously missed. Safety from the chaos like a break in a storm. A high of anxiety clashing with the low of loneliness, now a clear horizon. He created everything I could need for a short time. What felt as only seconds, crumbled at the alarm. A sound that rang of despair - an interruption. Peace dissipated to the swell of uncertainty. His arms released me, and the chaos returned.

Baggage Claim

It's such a common phrase when thinking about an individual's past traumas. People will sometimes refer to it as emotional baggage: the things people carry around with them day to day, relationship to relationship; sometimes explaining how or even why a person behaves in any particular way.

I like to think of one's baggage like going to an airport. When getting ready to leave, you might not be packing your own bags. One or both of your parents may have been packing your bags for you, or maybe that guy that sexually assaulted you. Better yet, maybe a medical professional or Death themselves packed your bags. Maybe all the above had a hand in what goes into that suitcase of yours.

You know the suitcase I'm talking about the one that you dress up daily to venture into the world. Sometimes sleek with four rolling wheels, other times, a little more rustic with a zipper that broke oh so many years ago. Mine is a lime green, hard shell with vinyl stickers pasted to the sides of it, along with a matching fabric carry-on. No matter what the vessel might be, I'm thinking more of the contents within. Regardless of whomever may have contributed to what is now your luggage or even if you had say, it is your baggage to carry and manage.

Now that you're at the airport, you must always carry it with you. You aren't allowed to hand it off to someone while you run free. No. That would be irresponsible. Plus, your baggage will always find its way back to you. There will be people in a hurry or often just not paying attention that might bump into you and your bags. This interaction can go any number of ways. It's easy to just let them pass, recognizing that you only have control of yourself and what you must manage. It's also very easy to be more irritated. Why couldn't that individual pay more attention to where they are going?

A more unfortunate scenario is that something within your baggage gets dislodged or even breaks. The contents rattles loudly as you walk to your destination, sometimes you catch the stares of others in your peripheral. There's an odor now, and a liquid leaking from the zipper. You must stop to clean the mess up, rearranging the contents that you didn't even pack. You're in the middle of a crowded terminal crying with a smelly, wet bag.

It's easy to blame the person who bumped into you. How dare they not be more courteous of you? What a fucking asshole! Yeah! That person could have been more careful, but that's not the case. We can't change that. They also didn't know that anything could be knocked around or broken. You might not have had that knowledge to begin with either. Nonetheless, you must clean the mess up. That stranger isn't coming back to support you, and it's not the business of anyone else. I'm assuming that whoever packed such a horrific substance is also not going to help you either. Yet, security will eventually ask you if you are carrying anything for someone else.

You might feel on your own or overwhelmed, especially if this is the first time or two and you don't have the resources to get assistance. Sometimes it takes a professional team to come in and assist with the cleanup. My personal professional team is my therapist, medical doctors, and my best friend. For you, the team might look different. It's okay though. It will all work out: you'll get things cleaned up enough to go about your trip.

It's the next part that's important. You can take the time to collaborate with your team to unpack your baggage, clean up the mess, and figure out how to manage the contents. That, as a mental health professional, is what I always suggest to anyone. You could also just ignore the contents, leave the mess. It can be a problem for someone else to deal with. Maybe a future partner will attempt to clean it out, removing what has only festered and molded over – having become even more toxic than if it had been taken care of sooner. You could just demand people deal with whatever baggage you bring with you. If they don't like it, they can leave.

In the end, we might try to hand our bags off to another family member, significant other, or even friends who might be picking us up. You may even attempt to leave the bag in a ride share car, but the bags will always be returned to you. Your contact information is plastered to the side of it. However you choose to deal with your baggage, there are consequences. Pushing your luggage to someone else may very well push that someone away from you, or letting it fester may cause long-term harm to yourself or others exposed to the contents within. The point of all this is that, sometimes, taking care of your baggage is important. We all have decisions to make about how we manage our bags and how we engage with others who might be carrying the with or for us. The choice is yours, and you can always change your mind at any given time.

The Cheerleader

Her voice became ridged and cold, like that of a parent scolding a child. What lay dormant now boiled to the surface. A disdain for a person that saw through her veil, the elegant facade hiding pain and loneliness. She felt threatened from even miles away. Entire states separated the phone call, yet the mere mention of their name caused silence to echo louder than her voice. She saw them as a plague moving across what she claimed as territory. Her hate rooted like that of a fungus, feeding from pain of those closest. Their presence countered her ability to consume. A joy she once long held proud, the control she wore like a tiara. Her opinion weaned in power as consort and subjects alike find more intrigue in the genuine rather than the manufactured gestures of those wanting to control all around them.

Pivotal Moment

Looking back, it's weird to think of the connection we had even a couple months ago, let alone recall last year. It's also odd to reminisce on how it all fell apart. I can pinpoint the day I felt everything leave my body, and day to day became an uphill battle. It was the time you found me near catatonic after a panic attack, only for you to become frustrated at me because the apartment was a mess. That day, your actions identified that you would never protect me, all the while you played nice with criminals. I fought for a year before I gave up and retreated, though you gave up long before I laid down my sword. You were done before we had even been engaged. Once you realized you'd have to put effort into the relationship is when you realized the relationship wasn't for you. You distanced yourself from me, looking for every reason to blame me for your fear. Though, truly, you're only scared to face yourself.

Covert

You would speak ill about yourself to garner sympathy while pretending you weren't talking about all your friends with backhanded comments. You presented just the opposite of your outwardly friendly demeanor. You sought out control and deemed many as incompetent, though the weaponized incompetence was the wolf in sheep's clothing. You used tears and stress as an excuse to speak in coarse tones and throw tantrums.

Your friends have become nothing but pawns – yeses to your plotted perspective. You conveniently forget context because it would only provide poor lighting to the act you attempted to perform. A play titled *Victim*; a one man show of how rough life can be if you don't get your way and pretend everyone is out to get you. The reviews are in: it's thrilling until the second act, then it becomes predictable. Zero stars: would not recommend it for any audience.

The reason you never wanted to seek help is because you were in control the whole time. It makes sense why you hid away from discussing past relationships as though they were dark secrets. If you disclosed the past then you'd either have to admit fault or add to the web of your lies. You ran from me the moment I saw through the limelight of it all. It was all a novel I was willing to set aflame, and you'd rather flee like a criminal than go down with your sinking ship.

Prick
Joey
Pendeja
Asshole
Lazy
Humorous
Puta
Tasted
Nuisance
Reasonable
Soul

No Punches Pulled

Conceited
Empathetic
Aggressive
Passionate
Cabrón
Selfless
Worthless
Ambitious
Annoying
Strongminded

You tore me down to exalt yourself above me. The emotional punch to the gut – low blows. You couldn't just leave the compliment for me to accept and made sure to drown out praise by knocking me down and digging your heel into my side. You didn't want me to know what I deserve because you feared I might wake up from my daze and see I deserved better. So, you made sure to put me in my place, since you wouldn't want me to know my true worth.

Sadness

The feeling of loneliness blankets me like a quilt tucking me in. I lay next to you with a mile of distance between us. It doesn't feel like it's the same bed, same room, or even same existence all together. I know you're just as upset, though I lay here, back turned to you, trying not to cry because I don't want my sorrow to cause more annoyance than I've already created. It's times like these that I imagine cutting myself deep, falling from high, or letting myself submerge. If I didn't exist maybe, you could be happier. For now, I'll continue to whimper to myself.

What is Lonely

It's a blank space
where none exists:
thoughts evaporate
into nothingness
and even darkness flees.

Art

You used tapestries to cover the holes in your walls –
reflections of your insecurities and deceptions – using them
to distract as though the illusion wouldn't eventually dissolve
like paper when dosed with a torrent.

Tiptoe

Tiptoe,
We continue to play
With the words
We mean to say.

Not to offend,
Or push away;
We tiptoe around
Words that will stay.

Passion Fruit

You told me I was "too passionate." Odd, since I've never known passion to be a negative factor. Why should I turn a blind eye to the things around us, or pretend I don't see the injustices within the world? Why shouldn't I be passionate about caring for those that I'm close to, or protecting the things that bring me joy? Too passionate? The irony. The downfall of our relationship wasn't because I was too passionate, though, it was because you were too numb to open your eyes. You did not want to see the world for what it is. You knew if you gave notice then the acknowledgment would be a truly painful experience. So, you told me I had to experience the world alone. While I refused to tolerate in the name of passion, you hid away in the name of just wanting to pretend only you could experience injustices.

Freedom

For the vast majority of their life, they had been prisoner in a body that was not theirs, called the name of another, and shoved into a dark cabinet to not be seen. They pretended to be another person for survival, and functioned as though the zealots around them were friends and not the foe they tried to camouflage as. They went unseen, and under radar long enough; they chiseled at their restraints until they could break free. They shed themselves of a false identity, an inmate shedding a shackle and ran into the open space for the first time. They were told they took up too much space. It was true, they took up more room than they could ever have imagined. Why should they not fill a room to grow and celebrate the freedom bestowed upon them? Maybe the room is just too small.

Whoever you are

his

Sir

Boy

Hubby

Hun

Him

Emma

Son

he

Taz

Uncle

A Name

You told me you couldn't accept what I had chosen because I disregarded the name you had graced me with. No! I did not disregard a name you gave to me; I disregarded a name you gave to someone you wanted me to be. A person that never existed, a human shield I hid behind for over a score just to survive the ongoing wrathful tides of ancient beliefs forced upon me from generation to generation. I dare not even title them for the masses would scream of self-persecution, an uproar of avoidance and deflection. The name you gave me has a long history of shame and torment attached to it like a scout's sash, mere badges of abuse and neglect from challenges a child should never witness let alone endure.

What is the name for you anyways? That name only found its way to your lips out of anger. Any other time I was a sibling or pet; rarely the name you seem to cherish as much as you're expressing now. I was so frequently called "boy": just a gender spoken in hopes I would never be like "those people". Those people you didn't understand until I revealed myself to be of them. Those people you try so hard to be allied with but struggle to accept the one speaking to you now. You teach others about love and detest hate, though here you are as you try to hide the family in the crypt you've built for them.

I could never win an award for my acting of a cishet individual - the signs were all there. As long as I lied enough, occasionally pretended to show interest in the topics of masculinity, it seemed to be suitable. Even with my faulty performance, I still heard echoes of whispers from up the stairs and down the hall, questioning my identity out of fear. A fear like you had been harboring a monster, as though I would expose myself and devour all. Yet, you still passively attempted to tame the projected beast I so poorly pretended not to be.

Would it make you happier to know that the person, the name you so identify to me to be, wouldn't be alive right now if it wasn't for my own intervention. The number of times I've had to stop myself from seeking out an end are uncountable. My imagination runs wild. Thoughts of a barrel against my temple, or steel pressed to my wrist. The blade would not stain, but your memories of crimson would haunt questions of motive and denial of them not being a he.

I continue out of spite. I live just to prove a point, showing others to be wrong in their flippant judgements of what they know not. I can be more than a name I have laid to rest, as its protection is no longer needed. Another body fed to the earth as compost. So, while you mourn a name, I celebrate a life persistent on sprouting in barren lands. I must make sure that all those that can't accept are plagued with my presence. I'll be the weed destined into turn this desert a lush green forest.

I hope that someday you can look past a name and see that I'm more than letters jumbled into a title for casual address. I am more than a noise that is expelled from your mouth or a word that comes across your mind. I am a person to be cared for more than what you would call me. You can't hug a name, but sure as hell can embrace me. A name is only a figment, whereas I am matter. So why should my choice matter less than what you have imagined me to be?

Love Me

Love me for who I am.
Who I was is long dead;
you'll only mourn what used to be.

Love me for who I will be.
Not with breath held dreams,
for only I can find my perfection.

Love me with all that you have.
I will feel through the distance,
and know it is true.

Love me not for what I have,
but what I can offer you;
possessions are temporary.

Love me for what we will become.
We will conquer the world;
just a prince and your knight.

Peace

My concerns were labeled arguments; my suggestions were a grab for control. My emotions were overlooked or rewarded with sarcasm. My attempts to keep the peace were met with adversity, as the only perspective allowed was yours. There could be no treaty nor negotiations if your demands were not met. Though your demands accrued interested that could not be paid, so I eventually walked away because there was no chance for us to survive.

Puppeteer

You once told me
I had control over you;
yet, I have become
your marionette,
moving to your command
over my heart strings.

Façades

No one cares about
why the rainbow exists,
only that it is there.

In the same way,
no one cared it was fake,
as long as they smiled.

Quilt

My heart was a delicately,
woven patch work.
You pulled the thread
allowing it all to fall apart.

You Made Me Cry

Your words struck like pebbles to glass. What would seem insignificant to others fractured my foundation. Tears poured as the dam of emotions crumbled. The force of anger gave way to the release. Tear-stained trails led from eye to chin as those that continued to pool burned with the heat of smoke and ember. One might think I had placed my face near a flame, though here I sit replaying every conversation, each shared moment, like a vinyl you'd hang on the wall. You compare yourself to an onion, but the only similarity is that you made me cry.

I'm Sorry

Your apologies were as empty as your promises and worth
even less than the air exhaled to speak your words of
insincerity. Your body language betrayed your lies, as you
attempted to skirt around responsibility and the ways to
accept it. You held pride in the way you thought you could
avoid accountability, until I laid the path out in front of you.
Then the game changed to how you could best light the gas
as you thought you'd shed light on my insecurities while
pretending there was nothing for you to apologize for.

Insecurities

You isolated me
with paranoid questions,
hiding your promiscuous behavior.
You feared I would abandon you,
so you abandoned me first.

Your Love

Your love was a reward to be earned and I often did not meet your mark. So, you withheld it from me as though you had been teaching me a lesson on how to better pass your test. You loved me, but you didn't like me.

A class from your mother, who only loved you after downing a bottle, who now downs a bottle in an attempt to forget her indiscretions. A lesson from a former partner that would only love you if you lay down and take him.

These things you turned on me. When I refused to learn by your syllabus, you deemed me unteachable: thus unlovable. I became too much for you to manage. You sought a new apprentice before you even expelled me.

Woodwork

She was of beautiful craftsmanship, though bestowed to those who would never appreciate the greatness she had to offer. She had no choice but to allow them to carve their greed and control into her being, chipping away at the sanity she had left. She only ever wanted to be something they were proud of. Instead, they criticized and critiqued until one day she had been whittled to the point of snapping.

Left In Fragments

Time slowed to what felt like a mere fraction of its normal speed. The glass award glided through my fingers. The sound of glass crashing against the floor broke the trance we were held in. The intentional soft toss led to the unintentional shattering. I immediately regretted my actions when I saw in your face that you'd no more leap to save what you demanded of me than you would leap to save me.

Time caught up to itself as what had once been whole now shattered across the kitchen floor; scattered shards sparkled in the dim light of the kitchen as tears poured down your face. Memories of screams and broken dreams played in your mind, like a movie on the big screen that could be seen in the gleam of your eyes.

The symbolism was spot on - like my heart and our relationship – we, too, were only shards of glass at this point. The word "whole" could never describe what we had become. It was that shattered glass which cut apart what little we had still connecting us. My one act of aggression was the last nail in the coffin. We both knew that night there was no going back; no fixing the hurt of lies, cheats, and now the way I smashed what wasn't even mine.

Gambled

I sacrificed everything
to play a risky game,
caring for you.
All the while,
you sacrificed me,
caring for those
who would cause you pain.
I played a stupid game,
and won no prizes.

Failed Foresight

It was a feeling
like none before.
As though we were
destined for more,
but now I sit alone
with nothing to show for.

Fooled

I trusted you as I did him;
each ended the same:
all I own packed up,
and your phones rung
with the names of others.

Weather

The pitter patter of rain splashes against the window, as my fingers touch the glass. Gingerly, I glide my fingertips down the glass, dividing the condensation with a clear view of the precipitation. Each new drop of drizzle, which spits on the glass, is met with a similar feeling in my heart. If my heart could cry, it would be sobbing. As the sky overflows with its collected waters, so does my heart.

Dreaming

Sometimes I close my eyes tight,
hoping that when I open them
it will all happen to be a fever dream,
though I can't close my eyes any harder
than I already have tried
and the pinches still feel too real.

Unfortunate Endings

She invested all her time
into a man who was
slowly eating away at
everything she was.

If only she had taken
up a hobby instead:
her paintings would have
brightened dark rooms;
hand sewn quilts would have
warmed loved ones;
fresh, hot meals
could feed all she knew.

In the end, she only found
herself to be tired and alone
with no time or energy
to do anything else but
simply exist as the woman
who could have been more.

Instinct

It's a constant need
to drive away from this
nowhere in the search
of somewhere to belong.

Part Four

He Used To

Look at me the way he used to. It was a face like a child in a toy store. An expression of joy so genuine; a state of disbelief that I could be real. A look of gratitude.

Hold me the way he used to. One arm under my head as the other wraps around my chest. Embrace me tight against your body. Whisper to me words of safety and security.

Kiss me the way he used to. Lips parted and pressed against mine. Our tongues greet each other as the sound of air escapes from our mouths. I'll caress your cheek with my hand like I had done before.

Faded

Do you ever wonder
what could have been,
or where I am?
In this very moment,
have you forgotten,
or do you pretend
I no longer exist?
Have I dwindled?

Even Now

I've had closure many times over, all leading to the same thing: you just didn't want me. Instead of cherishing me, you barely tolerated my presence. Though, I still find myself missing you on cold nights, wishing I could witness that smile as it had once graced your face. I know now what you've said all along, we could never be. While that rings true, especially after all is read to you, I still miss what I had long imagined to be a partnership worth keeping. In the end, I still catch myself with tears pooling beneath my eyes as our song plays, and hoping things could have changed. Yet, the past is sewn into the fabric of destiny, and our threads are knotted off separately.

Please Stay

Love spins
as a rotating door,
letting some in
and others out.

Some come to stay
making a home,
while others part ways
in silence.

Window Waves

Our eyes meet through windows to exchange smiles and excited waves. Though, those moments of bliss vanished after my words struck your core. I don't know how to apologize, so my gaze is never met, and my waves go unseen each day as you pass my window.

Bitter Truth

You made me reflect on my desires and truly think on the reality of my future. We probably will never be together more than we are now or in a deeper embrace than we had been the other night. Our time is limited, and I know neither are at fault, for both do not have control.

Repetition

They forced a love that ticked slowly to an explosion; as loved ones mourned their losses and chaos settled, the clock reset, and the ticking began once again.

Pride and Joy

You always have been proud of your mouth. You found a use for it, stroking egos and telling lies. You were jealous when I found someone who used their mouth far better than you could even imagine. He communicated genuine thoughts instead of blowing every guy he could find.

A Breakdown

The sound was not one heard around the world, or even within their own building, but only in the welling tears that pooled beneath their eyes. The final couple blows to a fractured soul, now laying in pieces across the fabric of time and space.

Small pieces, from similar feelings as a teenager, dust over North Carolina, circa 2009, like a fresh dew. Others were found scattered across King County - a trail of love and loss; lust and yearning. Some found in a tiny town in upstate New York, where if one goes to find themselves then they are only doomed to lose themselves further. All glimmering like gems in a riverbed of sorrow.

With an aerial view, the pieces could be mapped like the stars. Though, it wouldn't take a fortune teller to read that palm, nor a deck of cards to predict what was next to come. It could easily be seen in the glossed over eyes, the husk of flesh and blood. All that was left was the shell of a human, strong for everyone but themselves.

Bittersweet Memories

She hated the years of pain -
the control, the abuse -
but she still loved the man
he once was long ago.

Nightling

He stalked from perches and shadows, ultimately just wanting solitude while still vicariously living through those who actively participated in the mundane. He infrequently wandered to the crowds, most curious if his imaginative mind matched with that of lived experience. Though, he was often disappointed after returning to his dark corners out of fear of those who have been unkind.

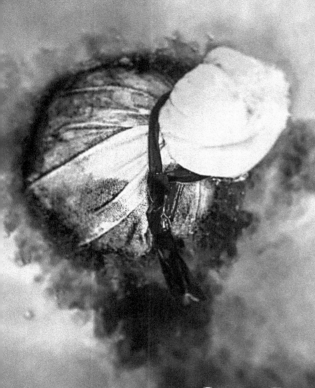

Love Bomb

Bomb me with your love and destroy my walls.
Devastate the boundaries I've set up to protect my emotions.
Tell me you love me only to inform me we will never be.
Watch as I collapse to my knees in surrender.
You have ravaged me once again.

Edmonds

Do you remember the day we drove to the north?
The deciduous trees transformed the evergreen
groves with speckles of reds and yellows, a blaze
of color to the dense foliage of green. The road
wound through the hills like that of a snake
moving from her nest to a sun-heated rock to rest
for the afternoon.

Do you remember the day we walked through the
town? The warm autumn sun danced with the
cool breeze of the waterfront as we strolled the
boardwalk. Light from the clear sky glistened
against the tide that gently sloshed onto the rocky
beach while little jellyfish wandered lost in the
harbor's depths.

Do you remember the day we sat at that little
cafe? We drank our chai as we had many times
before in many other venues, though this time
was different. The smell of dried seaweed filled
our lungs as we breathed in deeply, exhaling into
our seat, eyes closed, and we found a moment of
peace from the cluster of sounds about us.

Jenga

I strategically make moves
removing this piece here,
and the one right there,
hoping life will crash
into a perfect mess
of him and I.

Grim Departures

Every time he leaves,
a little of my soul dies
with the parting of our lips.

Dear Beau

The distance was too far for his feral lust to fully commit to you, so he had me as his casual comfort. He wanted to exclaim his 'I love you's as he rushed through mountain passes to see you, like a kid attempting to play Red Rover. He ran directly into yet another relationship with ambition to forget me in the process, though forgetting me would be too substantial of a task for him to accomplish. He adored the way I conveyed a sense of safety and security, while you strained to convey much at all. It was a bitter taste of irony as the same communication that he desired from you was the communication he would never provide to me. So, while you explore the mountainside, I explored his bed. You called him your boyfriend, and he called you just another man.

Drunk

Your kiss is an aged wine:
too good to pass up.
This drunken feeling
is one I would rather resist.

I Can't Breathe

Your presence was that of a thick smog, blocking out clarity and making me question my surroundings. Reality was distorted, my senses numbed. I lost sight of the good in front of me as I choked on your toxins – a decay to my brain. My judgment lapsed until you decided I was no longer worth keeping. You had no more use of me.

Venom

You told me we were toxic,
though, it was your venom
that was the catalyst for change.
No antidote or relief from pain;
life slips away as I beg for mercy.

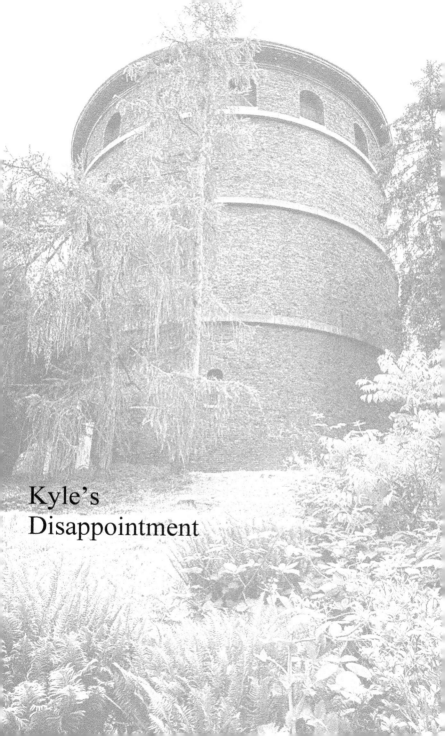

Kyle's
Disappointment

I supported you through sickness, job changes, and the deaths of friends. I sacrificed work hours to care for you when bed bound. I was there for you through each dark night of panic attacks and bandaged your cuts after you had applied them. Your biggest regret was that you hadn't supported a friend in their final moments of grief.

I told you I had a plan to end it all that very night, and you found yourself in a pit of rhythm and bass. I found myself screaming melodies of sobs to the harmony of meows from the being next to me. My life is owed to a cat, while your life wouldn't have continued if it hadn't been for my care.

Cleansing

Blood poured from the slit
along my wrist:
a letting waterfall,
draining memories
of days you stole.

The thick fluid
drip into the basin beneath,
leaving crimson reminders
of the pain needed
to rid myself of you.

The Last Spiral

Your words left me spiraling, only to be suddenly stopped
and told to walk a fine line between insanity and dignity.
Destined to stumble and fall right back to square one of
questioning my reality and what could be. You and I both
know the obvious answer is one we refuse to acknowledge,
so you go on avoiding, and I go on rationalizing.

Good Riddance

I asked you to take out the trash,
and you never returned.
There's no reason to be offended.
The bag fits; you wear it well.

Great Expectation

You buried the lead with false hope while I tried to bury the hatchet used to strike me down. You covered me up and hid me away. The only death left is yours. So, I now wait impatiently to dance on the graves of your lies and cheats, celebrating that in the end, my self-preservation is what kept me alive - while knowing you won't survive.

Fuck Boi

Our long silence broke with a message to reconnect past flings. We could be together only when it was suitable for you. Dodging written plans and providing excuses, gaslighting me to seem as though you were thinking of my best interests or that I was asking too much of you.

All I wanted was mutual respect and shelter, and you were looking for a warm body to jump into bed with. I was always the one to reach out first, the one that had a desire to spend time with you. You were angered when I called you on your disinterests, then lied even to yourself about actual intentions.

I wanted more than just a good time in bed, but that's all you saw me as. I was made a convenient toy to be used at your leisure then set aside so you could go on with your exploits of finding others at a discounted rate. I just waited for the text asking for those bursts of intimate exchange.

Do you wanna fuck me sometime?

The Price We Pay

You get what you paid for
with the currency as effort.
Though, if easy is the filter,
quantity will be the guarantee
and quality will allude you.

A Lesson on Effort

You want the things
you can't have,
discarding those
right in front of you.

Your effort is lacking
for the things that need it.
You want what's easy,
though easy doesn't provide
the quality you desire.

Nothing

Words dangle from my tongue
as I attempt to protect what is left
of the heart pinned to my sleeve.

Uncertainty makes me ache;
agony turns within my stomach,
and anxiety isolates me from you.

I want to tell you these feelings,
but I sense them to be mutual
only in the dream where we met.

Radio Silence

I fell asleep listening to our song, waking to nothing but the white noise of your absence. Now conversation barely scratches the surface as words like "fine" and "tired" are tossed about. Talking with you has become like talking into a can without a string: my words are lost to the abyss.

You Broke My Heart

Like autumn leaves so easily crushed, they crumble with the crackling beneath your feet and turning to dust in your hand. Once alive and thriving, until the tides turn, and seasons change. A vivid green shifts to a brown, eventual fodder to feed the next generation.

I can only warn of the hurt that can be caused for trusting a love that didn't love in return, or the pain of betrayal of someone whose actions target in such intentional manners. It's an experience that can only be firsthand, and not one from ink on pages or pixels on a screen.

Even with the passing of time, I don't regret ever sharing my love with you in the unconditional manner of my ways. I do, however, regret not loving myself enough to have let you go sooner. You see, while you are just a speck in the large image of who I am, I am always going to be with me.

Somewhere Else

I know there's a timeline where our actions didn't wear each other, and we would still be pinned in a passionate embrace. A universe where neither wakes up alone nor with another, but with each other. A place where we still shared a love like that of our best days together. Even our lows would be highs as we offer a sanctuary of grace from shame.

Now is not that time, and here is not the space. The reminder I have every morning when I don't wake to your face. The pain I feel fuels the resentment I have for how we are no longer together. I live my days slightly jealous of a self that only exists in theories. Though, I'm happy for us in that far off land. The one where we did everything right for you to still be my man.

Sober

Leaving you was many
long nights begging for death.
I only needed a smidge
or even a sip to help the pain.
It was for the best
to rid myself of you.

Runner

You did what you do best: run. You ran away from commitment, though you were the one setting the rate. You ran away from responsibility as you attempted to share in your blame. Sharing is caring except in times where you don't want to acknowledge the wrongs you've committed. You ran from my love the moment it wasn't easy because you thought love was a butterfly in your gut.

While you ran away from me, I chased thinking it was a romantic game of tag. Though every time I touched you, I was disregarded. You ran to acquaintances to moan of situations you created but couldn't find the rewind or undo options. You ran to men for empty sexual contact. You'd only come back to me for brief moments of joy only to run away again when what we shared was too real.

The Piper

You guided me to darkness.
I had been sleepwalking by your side.
You claimed my energy as your own.
I was drained by your spell and silver tongue.
You led me to my downfall.
I picked myself up from the thorns I fell on.
You left me alone in the wilderness.
I have since woken from the curse.

Slugger

Knowing I'll always protect my own, you only saw the fighter in me when I wanted to be a peacekeeper. You had the knowledge all along of how slowly you were hurting me, so you were prepared for the rage that would eventually ensue once I discovered my own self-worth. What you couldn't predict was my stern words being in written form and hitting you harder than I ever could with a bat.

Anew

You tied me to the tree
with your spiteful tongue
and set me aflame.
I now glow with a passion;
I know beauty will sprout
from what remains.

Wild Rose

You cut me out of your life like pruning thriving leaves from a plant. Wilted flowers only needing to be nurtured to create new buds, maybe a little more water would have helped. I hear it's good to talk with your plants, so maybe a little communication could have done the trick. Though here we are, leaves and petals on the floor. I was too much for you to keep, so you consumed my love for your own nourishment, as you neglected to maintain me in return. The remnants of what I had left were tossed aside. My spirit freed from the misuse of my offerings. Wild roses growing in a landscape they would have never originally chosen. I offer my beauty to others as our lives intersect for small moments, knowing that someday there will appear an individual willing propagate what I have to offer.

The Throw

I ran toward you like a bull to a matador, and sped past every flag like I was racing. I reasoned over every negative just to feel the serenity of being under you again. The presence and passion we shared reminded me of times long past when you maybe had once cared for me. Now, you've become no more than a specter that haunts my memories while removing me from your life as though I'm just last week's leftovers. Well, I can assure you, those leftovers are safer than the way you fish lined me to and fro until it was easier for you to cut me free than to keep a prize that would require earning.

Freed

Held captive by you,
My words never saw the day.
Your curse has broken,
Now these words flow
To mend a torn heart.

I

Became

a

Reflection

You unloaded your luggage and unpacked your bags, throwing the contents to me. You demanded I care for your trauma, and I carried it for you until we became spitting images of each other. Each day I saw less of myself in the mirror as I began to appear more and more like you. As your shame became my shame, we became identical: indistinguishable. You pelted me with all your insults because I was the closest looking glass you could find. You skipped over hurtles while I stumbled, then blamed me for embodying the paranoia you felt. It's amazing that in only a few short months of relinquishing your trauma, I reverted to a similar me from before I met you. Though this me will always hold new scars from wounds that have been dug into my skin with the most mundane objects, like the cuts you engraved on yourself.

Bleed Out

My heart once ached
to be attached to you.
One soul, one mind, one love
to take us to the end of time.
Our time has run dry,
and my heart has become brittle.
Not one word, song, or touch
of yours can heal such a fate.

Connections

I write because
I knew one day
it could be a link
to the two of us
coming together.
Though, now,
it is the stake
driving us apart.

Brush Strokes

You used to praise me for my art form. Compliment the way I manipulated words into scenes of grandeur. I often painted you, not only on canvas, but into my future. Now that the future has changed, and my blue skies have turned a sullen shade of gray, I continue to paint you as the man you present yourself to be. You controlled the subject, scene, and lighting, though you still criticized that my depictions of you were in poor taste.

Spite

You deemed me more spiteful than my truest core, and nothing motivates me more than being told I am not good enough. So, I'm leaning into the label as I want to at least earn the title being placard to my person.

Villainous

You claimed I aired our dirty laundry, but, like my hands, mine were clean to begin with. So, while your soiled jeans swayed in the wind, you told tall tales of my pettiness and your innocence. Singing rhyme, reason, and confusion like Snow White humming to all the woodland critters that would listen of how I was the wicked to be despised. Though, you always avoided the details that would add color to your cheeks or provide context to the lullabies. You demanded I be held accountable as though I had not been begging for ways to rewrite my wrongs. I can ensure, there are two sides to every coin, and while you rig yours with weight, I quietly wait for the opportunity to share all I have to say.

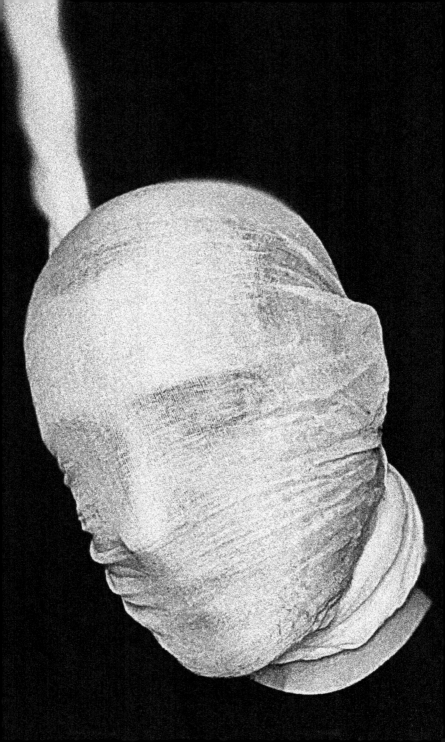

Vindictive

You would chant hopes of me finding happiness. I wish I could sing the same for you, though you drained me of it all. My hope for you is that you never find even an ounce of happiness. I want you to search high and low; no rock unturned, or creek uncrossed. I want you to believe you're coming close, as though happiness is just within your grasp. Just as your fingertips make contact, and you're about to take hold, it is quickly yanked away.

I would never wish physical pain, discomfort, or even death on you; though death is what you will want to beg for knowing that it's a far more merciful experience than paying your penance. I do long for you to atone for the psychological warfare you waged on me in the course of the time we were together. Holding me accountable for the trauma inflicted by past partners or parental figures; blaming me for the cuts you applied in the shadows. You demanded responsibility for your stressors and schemed the deliberate misuse of my emotions for the sensation of my body under the guise of mutuality. You played with me like a cat playing with its food, eventually devouring a meal. I was no more than easy entertainment in lonely hours.

I hope you never find a day a peace. I desire for you to toss and turn, unable to sleep at night. No, I don't want you to be plagued with thoughts of me - that would be a bit conceited and falls more in your wheelhouse. I just want life to always have a new huddle for you to crash through as though a door be painted to a brick wall. When one door is fallacious, another is a trap to fall down.

I conceded. We weren't destined for this life, and I believed we'd see each other in the next. I can only hope I get to witness your next life feel like quicksand, falling below any surface with no way to break for air. Lungs filled with tiny grains of misfortune that suffocate you to an eventual end. I want you to regret ever thinking you would get away with hurting me in any lifetime.

I dream you choke on your tall tales and mind games. Gasping for breath, your completion changing shades. I want these words to be the thing that comes across your mind. My face imprinted in the last image you see. Regret to fill you instead of oxygen. I fancy the thought of you cursing any and all gods for the misery brought upon you as the cost for agony you've caused.

You would tag me as petty, and it very well might be. Though, my little bit of spite is nowhere near as damaging as the effect you've had on me. You may tell me I should forgive and forget. Trust! I would happily like to at least reflect on memories with rose colored glasses, though there is no forgetting the impact a mere two years had on me. Forgiveness. Well, forgiveness is a hook you made me escape from all on my own and while I tend to catch and release, you are one that will remain lined. So, while you go about your life, struggling to make genuine connections and hurting even more people, I sleep peacefully knowing my wish for you is to never find happiness. The exact same happiness you offer as a consolation.

Fuck You!

Unforgettable

You thought you had wiped your hands clean of me months ago, but I found small cuts and crevices to crawl into. I'm the infection that now haunts you because to didn't bother to use soap to clean away the blood that had stained your hands. You can try to put me behind you, but there will always be a reminder that I'm not something that can be tossed aside and forgotten. I'm not dust to be swept under the rug, or a skeleton in a closet. I've never been one to be silent, so now that my lips are sewn close, my hands speak freely. I linger with interest compounding as the days continue and light that had once faded to night returns. You might have made friends with the block button, but I have made friends with those who know you. My experience will be words spoken to their image of you; they'll begin to question, and your answers won't align with what has been shared. You praise yourself for your ignorance and success on the backs of others giving you handouts, but I will celebrate knowing you will never forget the regrets of me.

Etches

I'm told to create new memories in places of old, but my brain is not a toy of magnet dust. Memories with you cannot just be shaken away. It's difficult to replace the laughter on city streets or skipping over bridges. I can't replace the rainy evenings in, and the sunny mornings out. There's no forgetting holding your hand in crowded places so neither would be lost, or hugging in secluded spaces to express the other wasn't alone. The echo of arguments speaks loud in the light of the buildings we lived in together, manufactured beacons that make my stomach turn whenever I'm forced to pass them. Then there's any time I'm held by another man I must remember that it's not your arms around me like all the times before. Erasing you from every sight I see would be asking for me to hide the moon from the night sky. Its soft glow will always be present like that of your shadow over my city ventures. I now leave this place knowing it will be the hard reset needed to wipe my slate clean. For if I ever return then I want so very much to be anew.

The Storm

The sky grew dark, not that of night, but of a gray only seen in the strength of moisture-soaked puffs above as they ready to release their collected bounty. The air became heavy, and a blanket of rain could be seen like a curtain rushing forward across the plains. A growl like that of a monstrous beast could be heard from above. The current pulls in and the funnel lowers itself to the ground.

You always loved the idea of chasing storms and found yourself in awe of the destruction that is done by such natural forms. I feared the day you would go chasing storms for yourself instead of just watching the footage of others. The concern was that you would not return home. What I could never imagine was you actively chasing the destruction of our home.

It wasn't with the sound of winds moaning loud in the ear or hail falling to the earth. It was you, the storm, chasing me out of your life. I became the storm chaser as you drew me in time and time again, only to spit me out like an undesired flavor. Anxiety billowed within me like the clouds themselves overhead. Regret overcame me each time I attempted to face you again.

I eventually awoke from my daze. What felt like a fever dream which I attempted to repress; the trauma lingered. Such things are not meant to be boxed away but released from the body. I let my desires go with the wind that once pulled me in, as I promised not to chase storms again. Since, the skies are clearer than before I'd known you.

The Rings

It rested on the wooden table amongst knickknacks and small mementos as dust began to collect like a peaceful snow of a winter evening. The hollow disk remained as a passive reminder that the one in possession had once used it to ask for another's hand. It had been returned only as a peace offering after the couple had parted and later reunited.

There the ring of metal and whisky barrel sat, as the former bearer occasionally eyed to see if there had been notice of it. Though, the ring rested untouched by the current owner. After many months of loud moans or bickering tones, and frequent silence from either party; the hand that once wore the ring had an opportunity to swipe it.

The ring now joined with its pair, reunited. Placed on a ceramic hand, cursing all who gaze, rests the pair. As a reminder that beauty and meaning can continue even after the resolution of association, the rings will someday lose their sting, and the wearer may bear them again.

In the meantime, a new metal disk has found its way to the hand. Not one of unification, but one of self-promise that their happiness doesn't need to be from any other, but from within their own experiences outside those of romance.

A Letter Never Sent

My dear,

I've been well. I know you'd be so happy for me. I know that's all you ever wanted. This is probably the first time I've felt peace in a long time. I can honestly say that it feels like the universe has finally smiled upon my existence with grace instead of vengeance. I know that's something I wish we could say the same for you.

I miss you. I think of you often. The way your grin stretched across your face as you tilted your head; the way you found laughter and joy in all your surroundings. You were such a goofball. You trusted so easily. You saw the good in people without question.

Thinking about you is difficult. I've been avoiding writing this letter, because it means that I must address all that I regret and wish I could have done differently. All those times I sacrificed you for the sake of someone else. All those times I was too scared to stand up for you, but instead hid away. When I thought I was keeping your safety in my foremind, I often missed the warning signs that danger was approaching, only to be blindsided later.

I wish I could say that I hate those that killed you, but I was right there with them. With no dagger in hand, I stood by and allowed them to strip you down and take your innocence. I wish I could say it was only one time, but I'd be ignoring the dozens of other opportunities you had been struck by fist and boot, bat and hammer, thrown across rooms as if you were a mere ragdoll being rejected by its owner when a new toy arrived.

I know I shouldn't feel at fault. What is a three, five, eight-year-old supposed to do when faced against someone three times my size and four times my age. You truly never stood a chance as you aged into a teenager, especially, when we had begun to see the world and the turmoil within.

The number of times I wanted to show you an act of mercy. I just wanted to end it all. I wanted you to pass peacefully from this life into the next like sinking below the calm surface of a drawn bath. Though, as we both know, I could never lift the blade or pull the trigger. I allowed others to do it for me, though they frequently botched the job. When you got cancer, I prayed to whatever powers may be that it would just take you. The world wouldn't have been any better off, though you would have been spared from so much grief. It would have been such an easy exit too.

Here we are, though, nearly a score later, and I'm writing a letter to be recited to a mirror, begging for forgiveness. I already know you understand. You were there with me, as I was with you. All you care about is that I am happy, and I can finally say that I'm at peace.

Self-Reflection

They are a rare explosion of humor and sass,
hidden within a shell of hardened scars,
who burns with a passion for adventure.

Star Dust

It is as though
you were chiseled
from a star, a gem
sent from heaven,
banished to earth
only to search for
others like yourself.

Forces

They are a force to be reckoned with. Their energy is chaos none can predict nor control. A free spirit many have attempted to tame, though even they do not succeed.

Eyes of passionate flames fueled by joy and sorrow; ever burning with the intensity of the sun, and only eclipsed by their tears. Heat radiates with such care and hatred.

Their smile: a sealed gate holding thought, hinges loose, often releasing a forked tongue and fangs. A mystery of either venom or antidote determined in mere seconds.

Their mind: quick and cunning. Wit and humor are the scar tissue over wounds, though exercised well to guard from farther damage. They read patterns in the unspoken words of body moment.

Kind is their soul. Even with all that has been inflicted, and against the wishes of those that tend to the withered garden, they continue to love.

Deep Blues

She'll grace you with a presence, not as if she had been handpicked, but like that of a twice divorced duchess. Royal in appearance, with markings like war paint, a natural makeup emphasizing her beauty, though as chaotic as they come. No one can find themselves in her way, and the knowing within her sassy expression is as though she'd be twice her age. Such fierce energy twisted into a pandemonium of gray striped fur. She'll sometimes simmer to a purring disk as your fingers run through the soft hairs of her back.

Pencil Lines

I erase you from my life
like a penciled sketch;
dusting away fine lines
of your past presence,
ignoring the scars left
deep within my paper.

To Hell with Them

Years of carnage
have prepared me
for the moment I left,
never to look back upon
the destructive forces
that once controlled me.

The Texan

His eyes are a sepia green. The same as a forest discovering new life after winter's death; a vivid reflection of the owner's lived experience. Once destroyed down to the roots, now saplings scatter across what had been barren, breaking through for first breath.

Time

I spent countless minutes crying over the thought of losing you, while there were hours confused by how I was in the wrong for loving you as I had. Days lost wandering this plane trying to pick myself up without you, and weeks being consoled by friends and family that you were the real problem. Months were spent trying to win you over until I finally lost all faith in the glory I originally saw in you. Now I'll spend years with far more joy than you could have ever provided to me.

Dead Muse

I try to use you as my muse so I might write something happier from times long gone, but now every nostalgic thought makes me question what was genuine or manufactured. The rose color has faded to black and white, and most of what I see now is your neglect. I raise my glass to the death of a muse. Here's to the next who takes your place. I hope they will inspire me to be the greatness you refused to see.

Fin

It ended the same way it began:
In a passionate texting conversation.
Though, the end was a different passion.
It was one of rage and resentment.
Frustration was the double edge sword,
And it struck us both to the ground.

Our death was like any other passing:
We flashed before my eyes.
I saw the good and great; bad and worse.
The time we skipped up a hill;
The time we fought on Halloween.
I saw it all in one quick flash.

You vanished just as quickly as you appeared.
I closed my eyes and drew my last breath.
I saw you crumble – a once solid being, now dust.
You fell through my fingers like beach sand,
A form none could recreate.
We were a piece of art now lost to time itself.

Stomach Bug

I've described writing as like being sick. There's this gut-wrenching feeling that something just isn't right. Letters swirl into words from deep within and eventually it all comes up: splattered against the page, word vomit. Sometimes it feels gross and smells a little bad. It will often leave a bad taste in others' mouths. The feeling afterwards is rejuvenating, like you can run a marathon or consume another meal. Your body feels refreshed from the awful feelings.

This experience – reviewing old pieces, writing new ones, compiling what is now this book – has been months long stomach flu. Constantly having the words in my mouth to upchuck onto paper with pen in hand, or little memos on sticky notes. Tears pour from my eyes as the force of the experience has been overwhelming at times.

My fever has broken, and much of what I have been throwing together has come to an end. I feel at peace with what has been said and developed. I'm at peace knowing this will go into the world, like rinsing it down the sink drain. It now leaves my hands and enters the world in not the most conventional of ways. One has to admit, this is a pretty sick way to think about it though – in a couple of different ways.

One Last Letter

The past year hasn't been an easy one. I've visited our grave a few times. Sometimes to cry, others to celebrate. There's been a séance or two. A few times I tried to just dig up the casket myself. I've been detained a time or so by friends for disturbing the peace, banned from even speaking your name. For a time there, I moved in secret, not unlike how you kept me a secret from most in your life. There was only one time I managed to get close to what we had. I swung that casket wide open and found that it was empty. You were nowhere to be found. Or… Well, or some other gravedigger managed to get to you first.

I have since placed that box back in the ground and sealed it with cement so as to never attempt again. My visits to our site have weaned in frequency. The memories that previously grew as flowers have been taken over by the weeds of your lies and cold tones, choking them like how they choked us. What was sweet aroma is now a bitter stench of decay. I curse at the site, spit on the stone, more than I ever mourn. If anything, I mourn what I thought we had. That is the realest loss. A death that came too soon. The person I had once loved, the human I once imagined you to be, was no more but a figment of the imagination. I've become disenchanted by the charm you previously offered as a façade to the corrosive being within.

I now leave this tomb settled in a forsaken field of memories buried away, just like you are now. Though, while I can mark the spots of others, I remove your stone and carve out our names from the plot. I don't want to be tempted further or forced with regret when I come to pay my respects of other memories long gone. I have sailed you down the River Styx, for you are of Hades now. I want no part of anything you have to offer.

Acknowledgement

I want to thank my family, especially my parents and sister, who have been amazingly supportive of my writing. Momma, you always said I'd write a book one day and you have been very encouraging throughout this process. Ivie, you put up with me talking about this almost nonstop and gave some great feedback and praise. You also kept the secret – so proud of you! Dad, you really solidified the purpose and reasoning by being an unknowing example of why I needed to share this work.

Morgan, you are the bestest friend I could have ever asked for. You put up with all my nonsense and held back a lot of I told you so's. I couldn't have done this without your reasoning, undying support, and your friendship. Also, you know too much at this point, so you're stuck with me.

I need to give a massive shout out to my other nerds: Fran, Fenton, Ethan, Marsh, Ben, Cesar, Jesus, and Addie. While you may not have known it at the time, y'all were such a big support for me. Y'all kept me grounded and provided friendship to me in times that I really needed it.

Ailish: You were the best of all my work spouses! Tell my true love, Jacob, that I miss him.

Heather. Gurl, you don't get out of this. I promise I won't be a *lil bitch* writing this. You have been a great friend, and I look forward to hearing (or reading) about your many lives.

Thank you to everyone that assisted in the editing and design of this passion project. Y'all truly helped make this a beautiful reality and I cannot acknowledge that enough.

Finally, thank you to all my past muses. I would not have ever found my voice in writing if it had not been for any of your failed attempts to silence me. It was me recognizing your efforts that made me realize just how powerful my words truly are.

About the Author

Alice Allis (They/Them/Mx) is your average, run of the mill, Millennial queer: waiting for the end of the world, but planning to survive the apocalypse to spite their mother. Writing is their way to process inner thoughts, their experiences, and the world around them – it is a far healthier coping mechanism than their standard humor.

Though they have called many cities 'home,' Alice now lives in Colorado with their two cats. They can often be found hibernating in bed, preparing to hibernate by cooking and eating as much food as possible, or doing nerd shit when not working and writing.

Index